The Daring Escape of Ellen Craft

by Cathy Moore

illustrations by Mary O'Keefe Young

Carolrhoda Books, Inc. / Minneapolis

All dialogue in this book is taken or adapted from conversations reported by William Craft himself in his narrative, *Running a Thousand Miles for Freedom: The Escape of William and Ellen Craft from Slavery* (1860; reprint, Athens, GA: University of Georgia Press, 1999).

The photograph at the top of page 46 appears with permission from *The London Illustrated News*. The photograph at the bottom of page 46 comes from *Black Foremothers: Three Lives* by Dorothy Sterling (New York: The Feminist Press, 1988). All attempts were made to contact the copyright owner.

Text copyright © 2002 by Cathy Moore
Illustrations copyright © 2002 by Mary O'Keefe Young

All rights reserved. International copyright secured. No part of this book may be reproduced, stored in a retrieval system, or transmitted in any form or by any means—electronic, mechanical, photocopying, recording, or otherwise—without the prior written permission of Carolrhoda Books, Inc., except for the inclusion of brief quotations in an acknowledged review.

This book is available in two editions:
Library binding by Carolrhoda Books, Inc., a division of Lerner Publishing Group
Soft cover by First Avenue Editions, an imprint of Lerner Publishing Group
241 First Avenue North
Minneapolis, MN 55401 U.S.A.

Website address: www.lernerbooks.com

Library of Congress Cataloging-in-Publication Data

Moore, Cathy.
    The daring escape of Ellen Craft / by Cathy Moore ; illustrations by Mary O'Keefe Young.
        p. cm. — (On my own history)
    Includes bibliographical references.
    ISBN: 0–87614–462–8 (lib. bdg. : alk. paper)
    ISBN: 0–87614–787–2 (pbk. bdg. : alk. paper)
    1. Craft, Ellen—Juvenile literature. 2. Craft, William—Juvenile literature. 3. Fugitive slaves—United States—Biography—Juvenile literature. 4. Fugitive slaves—England—Biography—Juvenile literature. 5. Slaves—Georgia—Biography—Juvenile literature. [1. Craft, William. 2. Craft, Ellen. 3. African Americans—Biography. 4. Fugitive slaves.] I. Young, Mary O'Keefe, ill. II. Title. III. Series.
    E450.C79 M66 2002
    973'.00496073'00922—dc21   2001000220

Manufactured in the United States of America
1 2 3 4 5 6 – JR – 07 06 05 04 03 02

In memory of Ellen and William Craft — C. M.

For you, Hal — M. O'K. Y.

Christmas was coming soon.

The Collins family was looking forward

to parties and presents.

For Ellen Craft,

Christmas just meant more work.

She was a slave in the home of
Master and Missus Collins.
Missus Collins had kept Ellen busy all day.
Ellen was grateful when night came.
At last, she could go home.

Ellen stepped out into the chilly night.

She was bone tired.

She walked along the shadowy path

to her tiny home.

Ellen shared a cabin

with her husband, William.

He was a slave, too.

Ellen hated being a slave.

Slaves had no freedom.

They had to do as they were told.

They could be bought

and sold like animals.

Even children could be sold
and sent away from their parents.
Ellen hated that most of all.
She had been taken away from her mother
when she was a little girl.
When Ellen married William,
she made a promise.

She would never have children in slavery.
No child of hers would be taken away.
Ellen and William wanted to go to
Philadelphia, a free city in the North.
But Philadelphia was a thousand miles
from Georgia.

Ellen and William had talked
about running away many times.
Now they sat by the fire
and talked once more.
Most runaways were caught
before they reached freedom.
They were dragged back to slavery.

They could be sold off or beaten terribly.
Sometimes slaves who fought back
were killed.
Ellen and William decided together.
They would rather die than be slaves.
They went over their ideas for escape.
All their old ideas seemed impossible.

Suddenly William grabbed Ellen's hand.
Her skin was light against his dark hand.
She could pretend to be white,
William said.
And William could travel as her slave.
Ellen squeezed his hand tight.
But quickly she saw a problem.
A white woman would never travel
alone with a male slave.
Ellen would have to pretend
to be a white *man*.
They would have to travel many miles
and fool many people.
It was their only chance for freedom.
They had to try.

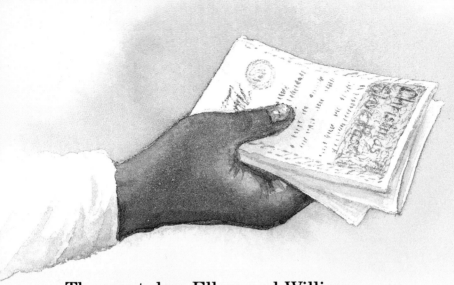

The next day, Ellen and William
asked for Christmas passes.
Some masters gave these out so slaves
could visit relatives in other places.
Ellen and William got passes to leave
on December 21.
But they had to be back
on the day after Christmas.
They had five days to get to Philadelphia.
After that, slave catchers
would start hunting for them.

Over the next few days, William and Ellen
secretly prepared for their escape.
William's owner had let him earn some
money by working for other people.
William would use the money
to travel to Philadelphia.
He bought a man's shirt
and a tall beaver hat for Ellen.
Ellen quickly made a pair of men's pants.
Her hands trembled as she sewed.

On their last night in the cabin,
they kept the lamp and fire burning.
William snipped off Ellen's hair.
Then she put on the men's clothes
and the tall hat.

Ellen looked in the mirror.

She still looked like a woman.

She wrapped some bandages
around her head.

They hid her smooth face.

She added dark glasses.

They hid her scared eyes.

Ellen had one more thing to hide.

A white gentleman

would be able to write.

But Ellen didn't know how to write.

Slaves weren't allowed to go to school.

So Ellen put her arm in a sling.

If she had to sign something,

she would ask someone to do it for her.

The bandages and sling

made Ellen look sick.

She would say she was traveling

to see a good doctor.

She would call herself Mr. Johnson.

Ellen and William spent the whole night

going over their plan.

Finally dawn came.

William blew out the lamp

and opened the door.

A cold wind blew into the cabin.

The pine trees shook.

Ellen shook, too.

She could never go out there.

She could never fool *anyone*.

It would be much easier to stay here,

by the fire.

But then Ellen pictured another fire.

She saw a fireplace in a home of her own.

She saw children gathered around it.

They were safe and free.

Ellen took a deep breath.

She lifted her chin

and pushed her hat into place.

Then she stepped through the door.

Ellen and William walked separately
to the train station nearby.
They met at the ticket window.
Ellen asked for two tickets.
One for herself and one for her slave.
The agent asked no questions.
He didn't yell, "Runaway slave!"

Ellen took the tickets
and held them tight.
She couldn't ride with William.
He had to ride in the railroad car for slaves.
Ellen would travel in a car
for white passengers.
She was on her own now.

23

White men filled Ellen's car.

They were smoking and chatting.

Then a white man sat down next to her.

"It is a very fine morning, sir," he said.

Ellen's heart pounded.

She knew this man.

He was Mr. Cray.

Mr. Cray had known Ellen

since she was little.

Would he recognize her?

Ellen turned her face to the window.

At first, she pretended she was deaf.

But Mr. Cray kept asking her questions.

Ellen made her voice low and calm.

She answered Mr. Cray.

He never guessed
she was a runaway slave.

In Savannah, Georgia,
Ellen and William boarded a boat
bound for South Carolina.
It was a cold night.
There was no place for black people
to sleep on the boat.
William had to sleep
on some cotton bags on deck.

Ellen stayed in a clean, warm bed.

Men snored in the beds nearby.

All night, Ellen lay awake.

She had been Mr. Johnson for one day.

She had four days to go.

When morning came,

Ellen wanted to hide in bed.

But she had to go to breakfast

and face the white men there.

William helped Ellen
into the dining room.
He called her "master" and "sir."
Ellen had to act like a master.
But she thanked William
for everything he did.
The men at breakfast
were curious about Mr. Johnson.
He was too nice to his slave, they said.
"You're going to spoil your slave,"
one man warned Ellen.

"You have to treat slaves like dogs.

You have to yell.

You have to scare them.

Otherwise they get proud and run away."

The other men agreed.

Ellen wanted to shout,

Slaves are not dogs!

But she just nodded.

She talked about her health instead.

In Charleston, William and Ellen
ate dinner in a hotel.
William had to eat in the kitchen
off an old broken plate.

Ellen was served by two slaves
in the fancy dining room.
She had to act like Mr. Johnson.
But she thanked them kindly
and handed them extra money.
Soon it was time to go
to the ticket office in town.

Ellen asked for tickets to Philadelphia.
The ticket agent wanted to be certain
William belonged to Mr. Johnson.
He knew that some white people
helped runaway slaves.
They pretended to be a slave's master,
so the slave could travel to freedom.
The agent gave Mr. Johnson a form to sign.

Ellen pointed at the sling.

She said she couldn't use her arm.

Would the ticket agent

sign the form instead?

The agent refused.

He didn't do favors for strangers,

he said.

Ellen didn't know what to do.

Finally, a man from the boat trip
said William was Mr. Johnson's slave.
Someone signed the form.
Ellen and William were one step closer
to freedom.

For two more days, William and Ellen
traveled by boat and train.
Ellen lay awake each night.
She worried about getting to Philadelphia
by Christmas Day.

On Christmas Eve, Ellen and William

arrived in Baltimore, Maryland.

They needed to take only one more train.

Once again, Ellen got into a car

for white passengers.

William walked to the car

for black people.

Then someone tapped him hard

on the shoulder.

"Where are you going, boy?"

a train officer said loudly.

"To Philadelphia, sir," William answered.

"I'm traveling with my master."

"Well, you'd better get him into the office,"

the man said.

"You have to get approval first."

William and Ellen walked to the office.

They tried to hide their fear.

Would they be captured

so close to freedom?

The railroad officer looked serious.

He wasn't going to let any slaves

escape to the North from his station.

He wanted proof that William
really belonged to Mr. Johnson.
Ellen said she didn't have any proof.
The officer asked if Mr. Johnson knew
anyone in Baltimore who could help.
"No," Ellen said.
A crowd had gathered outside the office.

Ellen tried hard not to show panic.

What should I do? she thought.

What would a white man do?

A white man would not be afraid.

A white man would be angry.

He would demand better treatment.

So Ellen did something

a slave could never do.

She stood up for her rights.

"I bought tickets all the way

to Philadelphia," she said angrily.

"You have no right to keep me here!"

The people in the crowd agreed.

Just then, the bell clanged.

It was time for the train to leave.

The crowd watched the train officer.

"I give up," he said finally.

"I suppose it's all right."

William and Ellen hurried onto the train.

Ellen took a seat by a window.

Outside, she could see

only cold, black night.

In a few hours,

it would be Christmas Day.

The train ride seemed to last forever.

And Philadelphia was nowhere in sight.

Early on Christmas morning,

Ellen saw lights in the distance.

It was Philadelphia!

As soon as the train stopped,

William and Ellen climbed off.

After the rolling, rocking ride,

the ground felt solid and still.

It was safe ground.

It was free ground.

Ellen looked around at the other passengers.

People were laughing

and hugging their families.

We can be a family now, Ellen thought.

We're finally safe.

We'll never be slaves again.

Ellen took William's arm.

And together they walked

toward the free streets of Philadelphia.

An artist drew this illustration of Ellen Craft in 1851 for a story that appeared in the British newspaper the *London Illustrated News*.

This photograph of Ellen Craft was taken after she and William had fled to England.

Afterword

After a rest in Philadelphia, Ellen and William moved to Boston, Massachusetts. William worked as a carpenter, and Ellen worked as a seamstress. They also joined the movement known as abolitionism. Abolitionists worked to bring an end to slavery.

William and Ellen gave speeches about their escape and about the cruelties of slavery. They wanted to convince people that slavery should end. Soon they were famous in the North—and in the South. The Crafts' owners found out where they were and sent slave hunters to capture William and Ellen.

The Crafts fled to England, where slavery was illegal. Truly safe, they could at last start their family. The Crafts had the first of five children in 1852. They also continued to give speeches. William even wrote a book about their escape. *Running a Thousand Miles for Freedom: The Escape of William and Ellen Craft from Slavery* was published in 1860.

After the Civil War, Ellen wanted to help the newly freed slaves. By 1870, the Crafts were back in Georgia. This time, however, they owned a plantation—and a school for black children. But money trouble and threats by whites made their work very hard. After about 19 years, the Crafts moved to Charleston, South Carolina, where they lived their final days in peace.

Important Dates

About 1826—Ellen is born.

1846—Ellen and William are married.

December 21, 1848—Ellen and William begin their escape.

December 25, 1848—The Crafts arrive in Philadelphia.

January 1849—William speaks publicly for the first time.

December 1850—The Crafts arrive in England.

October 1852—Ellen gives birth to the first of five children.

April 12, 1861—The Civil War begins.

April 9, 1865—The Civil War ends.

December 6, 1865—The Thirteenth Amendment officially outlaws slavery in the United States.

Summer 1869—The Crafts return to the United States.

1872—The Crafts buy a plantation and start a school for African American children in Georgia.

Around 1890—The Crafts move to Charleston, South Carolina.

Around 1891—Ellen Craft dies, followed by William.

Bibliography

Bolden, Tonya. *And Not Afraid to Dare: The Stories of Ten African-American Women.* New York: Scholastic, 1998.

Craft, William. *Running a Thousand Miles for Freedom: The Escape of William and Ellen Craft from Slavery.* 1860. Reprint, Athens, GA: Univ. of Georgia Press, 1999.

Quarles, Benjamin. *Black Abolitionists.* New York: Oxford Univ. Press, 1969.

Sterling, Dorothy. *Black Foremothers: Three Lives.* New York: The Feminist Press, 1988.

Sterling, Dorothy, ed. *We Are Your Sisters: Black Women in the Nineteenth Century.* New York: W.W. Norton, 1984.